LEGACY CULTURE

ADVANCE PRAISE FOR *LEGACY CULTURE*

"While talent certainly plays a major role in athletic success, culture is what determines how well and how consistently that talent performs. Culture is the key to maximizing chemistry and cohesion and is the foundation to long-term, sustainable success. This outstanding book shares the key elements of building a winning culture for any team!"

ALAN STEIN, JR., AUTHOR OF *RAISE YOUR GAME: HIGH PERFORMANCE SECRETS FROM THE BEST OF THE BEST*

"This book brings together all the elements of what an ideal culture would look like in a team and athletic program."

EDGAR SCHEIN, PROFESSOR EMERITUS, MIT SLOAN SCHOOL OF MANAGEMENT, CO-AUTHOR WITH PETER SCHEIN OF *HUMBLE LEADERSHIP* AND *THE CORPORATE CULTURE SURVIVAL GUIDE, 3RD ED.*

"*Legacy Culture* is a must-read for everyone, especially coaches, athletes, and those that work in a group setting. I believe the precepts portrayed here are valuable for today's society. Having the privilege of coaching Ron Monack makes this book personal to me. I know how passionate Ron is about living the concepts he explains in *Legacy Culture*. I highly endorse this book and hope it impacts you and others as much as it has me."

STEVEN E. SNIDER, FORMER ASSISTANT MEN'S CROSS COUNTRY AND TRACK COACH, SAINT VINCENT COLLEGE

"In *Legacy Culture*, Ron Monack provides a road map for coaches and athletes looking to develop a winning team culture. Using Schein's model of organizational culture as a framework, Monack details the Assumptions, Values, and Artifacts that form the structure of a successful team. This book is a valuable resource for coaches and team leaders committed to building a culture that enables all team members to reach their full potential."

DR. ANDREW HERR, ASSOCIATE PROFESSOR OF ECONOMICS AND HEAD CROSS COUNTRY COACH, SAINT VINCENT COLLEGE

"Understanding the three levels of culture is an important endeavor for any leader, regardless of whether you seek to influence a business, a nonprofit organization, or an athletic team. In *Legacy Culture,* Monack skillfully leverages these levels to suggest an ethical approach to coaching based on his personal experiences."

DR. MICHAEL URICK, GRADUATE DIRECTOR, SAINT VINCENT COLLEGE; MASTER OF SCIENCE IN MANAGEMENT OPERATIONAL EXCELLENCE

"*Legacy Culture* is not only a guide for coaches and athletes, but a guide to life. This book combines all the elements that it takes to build a strong culture. As a coach myself, I look to implement, as well as build upon, these principles."

SHAWN RAUSE, YMCA DIRECTOR OF SPORTS AND WELLNESS, GREENSBURG, PENNSYLVANIA

www.mascotbooks.com

LEGACY CULTURE

For more information, please contact:
Mascot Books
620 Herndon Parkway #320
Herndon, VA 20170
info@mascotbooks.com

Library of Congress Control Number: 2020913267

CPSIA Code: PRV0921A
ISBN-13: 978-1-64543-395-8

Printed in the United States

To my mother, Mary; my father, Ron; and my sister, Megan. Your support has allowed me to chase my dreams.

To Coach Herr and Coach Snider, for caring for me, never giving up on me, and demonstrating to me what it means to be a servant leader.

To Dr. Michael Urick, for your support and for exposing me to Dr. Schein's work. This book would not exist without you.

DEVELOPING THE NEXT GENERATION

LEGACY

— OF STRONG ETHICAL LEADERS —

CULTURE

WHILE WINNING CHAMPIONSHIPS

RONALD MONACK

TABLE OF CONTENTS

INTRODUCTION

DR. EDGAR SCHEIN IS A world-renowned social psychologist who has studied culture and leadership extensively. He is well known for developing a three-part framework to explain culture: Assumptions, Values, and Artifacts[1]. The Assumptions of a culture are the deeply held beliefs that are so engrained in the individuals that they can go unnoticed and are not often talked about[1]. The Values of a culture are the beliefs, goals, or ideals of the members of the culture that might not necessarily manifest but are a result of the Assumptions[1]. Values are the standards that guide an individual's behavior on a daily basis[1]. Finally, the Artifacts of a culture are the tangible manifestations of the Assumptions and Values[1]. Artifacts commonly take the form of behavior by the members of the culture. According to Schein's model, Assumptions are what drive the creation of Values, and Values drive the creation of Artifacts[1].

Athletics are a powerful tool to develop and influence young individuals. Often, sports coaches want to develop their athletes into strong ethical leaders, but they may have difficulty understanding how to bridge the gap between the sport they coach and their athlete's daily lives. The answer for how to create that bridge lies in the *culture* of a team set forth by the coaches. In order to help coaches achieve this goal, I developed Legacy Culture, inspired by Dr. Schein's model. Legacy Culture is a tool that coaches of all sports can adopt and utilize in order to achieve their goal of developing the next generation of strong, ethical leaders while still striving to win championships.

In today's society, we see scandals being reported involving colleges and organizations. In response to this behavior, I wanted to do something to give others hope and make a positive difference to offset the negative stigma of athletics fostering unethical behavior in individuals. Legacy Culture is my way of giving back and leaving a lasting positive difference in the world. It can be adopted by any team and is applicable to everything from sports to business. Legacy Culture can be used as it is presented, but it can also be altered to meet the individual needs of teams and organizations. By adopting Legacy Culture, we can change the world by developing the next generation of young ethical leaders and strengthening the abilities of today's current leaders. It is important to remember that there is no such thing as a perfect organization, team, or culture. People make mistakes and it is people that make up cultures. Even after implementing Legacy Culture, problems still have the potential to occur. When executed correctly, Legacy Culture will help to mitigate problems, but will not eliminate them entirely. However, one of the great benefits of Legacy Culture is that it will prepare leaders and members of the culture to handle problems appropriately when they do occur.

Elements of a culture include shared understandings and beliefs among individuals. Culture can influence behavior which allows for the predictability of behavior. Culture allows us to study and understand behavior. Each team and organization has a culture. Culture is neither inherently good nor bad. It can promote ethical or unethical behavior. The type of behavior that is exhibited by individuals in any given culture is most often a product of the underlying beliefs in that culture[1]. In today's world we are bombarded with cynical stories of leaders in organizations partaking in unethical behavior— stories of greed, manipulation, abuse, and dishonesty. Additionally, we see professional athletes, whom so many young people look up to, engaging in unethical behavior off the field and sometimes displaying poor sportsmanship on the field. In an attempt to mitigate unethical behavior, promote the highest level of sportsmanship, and develop the next generation of young leaders of the world, teams can use the Legacy Culture as a tool to prevent the next scandal in college sports, the next act of domestic violence by a professional athlete, and the next case where cheating is uncovered.

You have heard the saying "winning isn't everything." This is true; winning is important, but it's not the most important element of athletics. Teaching young individuals through athletics to be productive, ethical citizens is the most important thing. One of the great benefits of Legacy Culture is that it develops the character of young athletes without foregoing the importance placed on winning. A team that is disciplined enough to adopt and live by the values of Legacy Culture will undoubtedly achieve success.

How Legacy Culture Should Be Used

It should be made clear that Legacy Culture is not a standalone, be all end all, cookie cutter way of life. It is a framework and philosophy that is intended to be applied to an existing culture. Team cultures are very diverse, but that does not make one culture better than another. Legacy Culture is not meant to detract from the healthy preexisting beliefs, traditions, or activities that teams already engage in; it is simply a tool that can be used by leaders looking to improve their team's existing culture. It is the responsibility of leaders utilizing Legacy Culture to determine the best way to integrate the principals of the Legacy Culture framework into their culture. Leaders should ask themselves, "How can the Legacy Culture framework best meet our needs? And what form will the Artifacts take in our culture based on the preexisting beliefs, traditions, and activities of our organization?"

It is important to understand the relationship among Assumptions, Values, and Artifacts.[1] Assumptions breed Values, and Values breed Artifacts.[1]

ASSUMPTIONS → VALUES → ARTIFACTS

When it comes to your team's culture, Artifacts are the most important of the three. Why? Because the Artifacts are the final product. How others will view you and experience your presence as a team is based on the way they perceive you through the five senses. The Artifacts are what give the Values and Assumptions power. For example, a person may have a strong belief (Assumption) that they want to be healthy and fit. This may cause them to form the Value that eating healthy food is good for them. However, the behavior (Artifact) that comes from this Value is the behavior of eating healthy. A person can have this Assumption and Value about eating healthy, but if they do not eat healthy foods consistently, this Assumption and Value become very weak and lose their meaning in the person's life.

In his work, Dr. Schein states that Values can be strong or weak and do not always translate into Artifacts within a culture.[1] This happens with sports teams and company cultures all the time. It is the common practice of saying one thing and doing another, which most people are easily susceptible to. Almost every company designs a mission and vision statement in addition to outlining their organizational values, but oftentimes they do not translate to the culture of the company. A culture is still present within the organization, whether it be strong or weak, but it may not be the culture a company aims for in their employee handbook. For example, a common misalignment of desired company values with the actual company values could be related to teamwork. Teamwork could be a desired value for the company culture, but in reality, the culture could be one in which members keep secrets in an attempt to outdo one another. The relationship can also go the other way.

ARTIFACTS → VALUES → ASSUMPTIONS

Intuitively, it might make sense that if you want to change, you must first change your mindset and beliefs and then the behavior will follow. However, this may not be the most effective way to alter behavior. It is more powerful to first change the behavior, and then a change in mindset and beliefs (i.e., Values and Assumptions) will be more likely to follow. This idea is known as "task alignment," based on the work of Beer et al. (2019). This idea involves aligning team member roles and responsibilities to be consistent with the mission, vision, and values of the organization. Through their research, Beer et al. found that companies that utilized a top-down approach to programmatic change—in which the leaders promote the mission, vision, and values of the organization—were less effective at bringing about change because there is a disconnect between the ideas they are trying to engrain in the culture and how they translate to behavior for each individuals role within the organization. Task alignment, on the other hand, is a bottom-up approach in which behavior is altered first to be in line with the desired values of the culture and then over time the values that are in line with the behavior being performed will become engrained in the culture. A great author of the twentieth century, C.S. Lewis, referring to the power our actions have in influencing our beliefs and habitual behaviors, once wrote, "Do not waste time bothering as if you 'love' your neighbor; act as if you did. As soon as we do this, we find one of the great secrets. When you are behaving as if you loved someone, you will presently come to love him."

It is important to talk about the Values and Assumptions of your culture with your team because it reinforces the "why" behind the Artifacts. The Artifacts will be the most important part of your culture because they are the final product. Mentioned earlier was the example of healthy eating. An individual can believe in eating healthily and want their body to be healthy, but if they do not choose to eat healthy foods, what good are their beliefs? As a coach, you can talk about the importance of sportsmanship and respecting your opponent, but if your athletes engage in trash-talking and taunting, it is clear that sportsmanship and respect are not valued highly enough by the athletes to connect with their behavior. Another way to think about this is a parent asking a child to clean their bedroom. The child may not want to do the chore and may even protest against it, but if in the end they complete the task and their room is clean, it is considered a successful achievement. For the sake of optimism, we can assume that as the child ages, they will come to understand the importance of having a clean room and no longer view the task in a negative light. As a coach you may have athletes that at first do not buy into the Assumptions and Values (the why) that support the desired Artifacts (the behaviors) that are expected of them. But if they respect your authority enough to follow through on performing or taking part in the Artifacts, then that is a short-term win for the team and the culture. It has been widely noted that organizational change is difficult, and it can take a significant amount of time to gain the buy-in from the members of a culture, but that does not mean it is not worth striving for. It simply requires strong leadership.

As a coach, establishing a relationship with each athlete is critical. One of the best ways to do this is by meeting with your team one-on-one either once a week or biweekly. In this conversation, get to know your athlete. Go beyond the sport by discussing their academics and personal life (at their discretion). The idea is to genuinely care about your athletes beyond the sport or activity that brings you together. Through dialogue, coaches and athletes build a relationship. If both partners are genuine and caring, this relationship will be built on trust. Establishing trust between coaches and players is an important part of any team, but it is essential for Legacy Culture to be successful. The answer to why this is can be best explained in the words of author Josh McDowell: "Rules without relationships lead to rebellion and discipline without relationship leads to bitterness, anger, and resentment." Without a trusting relationship, all efforts to inspire change through leadership fall short.

It Starts at The Top

In order for Legacy Culture to be successful, it must gain support from upper-level management of your team or organization. Without the support of both administrators and coaches, Legacy Culture will struggle to survive. Once a coach has chosen to journey down the path of adopting Legacy Culture for their team, they must develop a strong understanding of all three levels of Legacy Culture. Coaches must have the Assumptions ingrained in them and make those Assumptions the foundation of their program. They must understand the Values inside and out and display them to their athletes daily. Coaches must live by the Values and demonstrate the Artifacts through their behavior.

As a coach, you must accept that you have the greatest responsibility of all. You are the ultimate leader of these young men and women. Everyone makes mistakes, but coaches must understand that they set an example for their athletes. To violate the Values you stand for is to undermine Legacy Culture and put the faith and trust of your athletes into jeopardy. As a coach, you must understand that when times get tough and athletes want to quit or shy away from Legacy Culture, they will look to you, and as a coach you must be the one to remain grounded in your beliefs and overcome the adversity. Being the top leader of a group adopting Legacy Culture may come with pressure, but that is not meant to make coaches shy away from adopting it. Rather, it is a challenge that should be embraced with great optimism and zeal.

There are three key actions for establishing Legacy Culture and instilling the Assumptions, Values, and Artifacts.

- **Plan**: Communicate effectively as a coach/leader and understand how you are going to execute the three levels of culture. Changing or establishing a culture takes time, but understand that setting clear roles and expectations for athletes throughout the entire process is essential.
- **Preach**: Reinforce the Assumptions, Values, and Artifacts by talking about them on a regular basis with your team members. This comes back to the idea of setting clear roles and expectations so everyone knows what is expected of them.
- **Live**: Practice what you preach. As a coach/leader, you are at the forefront of the way of life you wish to see in your team. Everything you say and do will have an effect on how you are viewed and respected. Although there is pressure, you should not worry. All this requires is living a genuine life congruent with the beliefs you endorse. You are not expected to be perfect, but always own up when you make mistakes and strive to achieve the standard you have set for yourself and your athletes.

Outline of Legacy Culture

Assumptions	Values	Artifacts
Love of the Game	Legacy	All
	Positive Attitude	Camaraderie Best Effort Overcoming Adversity Maturity Teamwork
Desire to Become the Best Version of Yourself	Work Ethic	Best Effort Overcoming Adversity
	Grit	Best Effort Overcoming Adversity Maturity Teamwork
Ethical	Integrity	Transparency Maturity Servant Leadership Best Effort
	Respect	Camaraderie Maturity Servant Leadership Teamwork Class
Selfless	Family	Camaraderie Teamwork
	Unity	Camaraderie Teamwork Servant Leadership
	Humility	Camaraderie Best Effort Maturity Teamwork Servant Leadership Discipline
	Sacrifice	Camaraderie Maturity Servant Leadership Teamwork Discipline

ASSUMPTIONS

Assumptions of a culture are the deeply held beliefs that are so engrained in the individuals that they can go unnoticed and are not talked about often.[1]

LOVE OF THE GAME

THIS ASSUMPTION MEANS THAT WHATEVER you are naturally inclined to do, whatever you are involved with—whether it is a sport, game, business, or hobby—you do it purely for the enjoyment of being a part of that activity. It is not all about winning. You are simply thankful to have the opportunity to do what you love. You do not need to be paid to do what you do, but if you had the opportunity, being paid would be a bonus. You derive joy from participating in the activity that you love. This assumption fosters the values of Legacy and Positive Attitude.

What This Assumption Will Mitigate

This Assumption, Love of the Game, will mitigate members of your team taking for granted the opportunity that they have to participate in the sport or activity they enjoy. This Assumption will instill gratitude within members of the team, which will guard against arrogance and pride. It will also guard against putting an emphasis on winning above sportsmanship and character.

How to Instill This Assumption in Your Culture

As a coach/leader, talk openly about this Assumption in your culture. Reinforce the idea that although we care about winning, winning is not everything, then practice what you preach and live a life of gratitude to exemplify this Assumption. Steve Snider, a former track and field and cross-country coach at Saint Vincent College, was known for his catchphrase, "It's a beautiful day," and in saying this, he would constantly reinforce the Assumption of Love of the Game. Coach Snider would frequently greet his athletes this way at early morning and afternoon workouts. Of course, most of the time Coach Snider's catchphrase was not used in reference to the weather. In fact, he would say this most often to athletes who may have struggled to get out of bed in the morning or when the conditions for running were unfavorable outside. By saying this, his message to the athletes was not to check the weather report, but to reflect on all they had to be thankful for. In this case it was the opportunity to get better at what they loved (running) and enjoy the camaraderie of their teammates.

DESIRE TO BECOME THE BEST VERSION OF YOURSELF

IT IS ASSUMED THAT YOU want to be a part of whatever team, group, or organization you are involved with because you want to reach your full potential. This deeply held belief brings together the best people who are committed to a common goal. By developing your talents to become the best you can be as an individual working to maximize your natural talents, you will be helping your team become the best it can be. This assumption fosters the Values of Work Ethic and Grit.

What This Assumption Will Mitigate

This Assumption, Desire to Become the Best Version of Yourself, will mitigate laziness and complacency among team members. It will also discourage beliefs that fall in line with a fixed mindset[3]. This is to say that team members should find themselves believing they are capable of improving their skillsets beyond their current capabilities.

How to Instill This Assumption in Your Culture

As a coach/leader, openly talk about getting better each day. Put an emphasis on personal improvement by setting realistic, personal goals for athletes to achieve throughout the course of both the on and off-season. Exemplify this by living a life in which you are focused on your own personal goals and share them with your team, so you can be their example.

ETHICAL

IT IS ASSUMED THAT YOU want to be a part of your team by conducting yourself with the highest level of morality. You desire to do things the right way and will not cut corners. Behaving in an ethical manner comes before anything else. Behaving ethically is valued over winning. The desire to be ethical in every area of one's life breeds the values of Integrity and Respect.

What This Assumption Will Mitigate

This Assumption of Legacy Culture must be at the core of everything the team's culture stands for. Through the power acting Ethically has as an Assumption, and through the Values and Artifacts associated with it, it will mitigate instances of lying, cheating, stealing, corruption, and other inherently selfish behaviors that may put others within and outside of the team's culture at risk for abuse or harassment at another's expense for personal gain. There are many examples of companies and universities that have been involved in egregious ethical mistakes: Enron, Southern Methodist University,

Pennsylvania State University, etc. It takes years to recover from these types of abuses and they are all the outcome of poor, unethical leadership. Legacy Culture has been created to prevent these types of ethical scandals or stop them before they get out of hand.

How to Instill This Assumption in Your Culture

Ethical is a term often used in a very broad sense. Every company wants to be ethical, but how much of this is fluff in their mission statement as opposed to a true sense of morality that employees strive for at all times? There are two recommended ways to establish Ethicality as an Assumption in Legacy Culture: 1) Preach the Values of Integrity and Respect and live out the Artifacts that are associated with these Values. 2) Insist that the opposite of what is ethical—corruption, abuse, harassment, cheating, etc.—cannot be tolerated and must be handled with swift and appropriate action within the team or organization.

SELFLESSNESS

IT IS ASSUMED THAT YOU enjoy participating in your activity, and you know you will derive personal benefits (friends, purpose, popularity, etc.) from being a member of your team, but you are not in it for yourself. You are committed to making the team better. You understand that the sport, team, institution, or organization that you are privileged to be a part of is bigger than yourself, and you are thankful to have the ability to participate in an activity you enjoy. This assumption breeds the Values of Family, Unity, Humility, Leading by Example, and Service.

What Selflessness Will Mitigate

The Assumption of Selflessness along with the Values and Artifacts associated with it in a team's culture will mitigate selfishness and entitlement among team members.

How to Instill This Assumption in Your Culture

Selflessness is an Assumption of Legacy Culture and is the foundation of multiple Values propagated by Legacy Culture. The best way to instill this Assumption into your culture is to talk openly about the Values it breeds and live out the Artifacts associated with each Value. Although each Value embodies the essence of Selflessness, arguably the most important one is Humility.

VALUES

The Values of a culture are the beliefs of the individuals of the culture as a result of the Assumptions.[1]

LEGACY

THE VALUE OF LEGACY MEANS the members of the culture understand that the team and the school or organization, regardless of level, is bigger than themselves. Being a member of the team is a privilege not meant to be taken lightly. Current team members must be mindful of both the past and the future. The past houses the great athletes and coaches who have come before the current team members. They paved the way to establish the program as it is known today. You owe it to them to try to exceed their expectations and continue the legacy they left behind. The future encompasses the members who will one day take your place as part of the team, whether it be players, coaches, or administration. You have the responsibility to set the standard for what is to be expected of the next generation. All of the Artifacts outlined in Legacy Culture are a tangible representation that Legacy is a Value in your culture.

As a coach, you will recognize that Legacy is a Value of your team's culture when the following Artifacts are present in your culture: coaches and players reflect on the members of the culture that came before them and desire to achieve goals greater than what was previously achieved in the hope of leaving the program better than how they found it.

Real World Examples

It is common for professional sports teams and university athletic departments to memorialize the legends who were once a part of their organization. You can typically find a location where plaques, trophies, statues, and commemorative photos reside. It is important to acknowledge the achievements of the past to set the standard for the future.

Why Legacy Works

Dr. Andrew Herr, the head coach of the men's cross country and track teams at Saint Vincent College, and Mr. Steven Snider, former assistant coach, believe in reflecting on the reputations and abilities of past athletes who have come through the program. Whether they were spectacular runners or outstanding students in the classroom, Coaches Herr and Snider would frequently reminisce and tell stories about athletes from the past. These stories immortalized the legacies of these former athletes within the program and set the standard for the athletes on the current team. It gives the current athletes an example to follow and is powerful because the individuals in the stories are real. Therefore, it makes their achievements of excellence feel attainable for the current team. Athletes are more likely to live up to a goal or standard when they truly believe it is possible for themselves.

POSITIVE ATTITUDE

THE VALUE OF POSITIVE ATTITUDE means that when you face adversity, you look for the upside. It is OK to acknowledge the difficult circumstances that may have set you back, but your focus should be on how you can improve and overcome the obstacles you face. You strive to maintain a positive frame of mind at all times. When you experience negativity coming from yourself or see negativity in others, you attempt to cut it off immediately. The Artifacts of Camaraderie, Best Effort, Overcoming Adversity, Maturity, and Teamwork are all visible evidence that Positive Attitude is a Value in your culture.

As a coach, you will recognize that having a Positive Attitude is a Value of your culture when you experience the following Artifacts in your culture: optimistic language is used among the members of your culture, members of the culture maintain composure in the face of adversity, they believe in their individual abilities and the abilities of others, and they view failure as an opportunity for improvement.

Real World Examples

Kayla Montgomery, a cross country runner featured on ESPN, was diagnosed with multiple sclerosis as a teenager. Her condition forced her to give up playing soccer, the sport she loved. After experiencing this devastating news that would change her life forever, Kayla had the option to move forward or wallow in self-pity. She chose the former and turned to running. Kayla faced her circumstances and refused to let them stop her from doing something she loved. She lost feeling in her legs and required someone to catch her at the end of her runs when she fully exerted herself. Her decision to focus on how she could turn her negative circumstances into a positive situation exemplifies what it means to embrace a positive attitude. Kayla had a successful high school running career, competing at both the state and national levels and winning championships. She then went on to compete at the division one level for Lipscomb University.

Why Having a Positive Attitude Works

Today's culture occasionally propagates the idea that a person should be happy all the time and it is not okay to be sad or depressed. On the contrary, it is healthy to grieve and experience sadness, but when these emotions have run their course, continuing to feel sorry for oneself will not improve a situation. When mistakes are made or adversity is encountered, the Value of having a Positive Attitude requires an individual to acknowledge the mistake and or unfortunate circumstance and move forward. Having a Positive Attitude is empowering because it forces one to focus on what can be controlled in this very moment. When athletes understand this principle and develop this mindset, they will be more inclined to act and come out of the challenges they face with resiliency.

WORK ETHIC

THE VALUE OF WORK ETHIC means that every day, everyone involved in your culture is trying to improve in all areas of their life. Everyone has the desire to maximize their talents. With the support of one another, each individual's full potential can be achieved. This Value is a staple of Legacy Culture. It signifies that although good and bad days are expected, 100 percent effort will be given each and every day to becoming better. When Best Effort and Overcoming Adversity become Artifacts in an organization or team, it is clear that Work Ethic is a Value of the culture.

If your team has a strong Work Ethic, you will see team members arriving early, staying late, and going beyond what is asked of them. Team members do not need external motivators because they care about their own personal development, their teammates, coaches, and school/organization.

Real World Examples

Michael Jordan is often regarded as the greatest basketball player of all time, but he did not earn this recognition without making great sacrifices. Michael Jordan was known for having a work ethic that was unmatched. He was willing to work harder than everyone else because he hated losing more than everyone else. He was known for practicing at his house before official practices, then staying after official practice had ended to further work on his skillset or basketball IQ. Michael earned the respect of others because not only was he the best player, but he was also the hardest working. It is rare that the best player is also the hardest working, but when it happens it is a recipe for success on any team or within any organization.

Why Work Ethic Works

Talent can only go so far, but work ethic can surpass talent. It is safe to say that most coaches would rather have a team with a dedicated work ethic than a talented team that is lazy or full of drama queens. A showing of strong work ethic in your athletes will command the respect of teammates and coaches, and this respect will lead to trust. Let your actions do the talking. Teammates respecting and trusting one another is a key to success.

Coach Herr and Coach Snider understood that their runners would not achieve a personal best every race and that not every workout would be the best workout of their athletes' careers. They understood that some days are better than others, but what matters is that athletes show up and put forth their best effort with the intention of getting better each day.

GRIT

THE VALUE OF GRIT MEANS that the members of your culture are not expected to be the most talented, the fastest, the strongest, or the smartest, but they are expected to have one intangible quality: that they never quit. Dr. Angela Duckworth defines grit as "perseverance and passion for long term goals[3]." Having Grit means you never give up. You take on challenges as you face them, and you adapt to them. You find a way to overcome the obstacles that you face, not only individually, but as a team. Members of the culture should understand that they are strongest when they work together as a team. Having a never-give-up mindset is a lot easier for a group to adopt rather than an individual alone. This will foster teamwork in your culture. Over time, Grit will shape the members of the culture into individuals who feel prepared to take on the world and face adversity by themselves long after their days of being a member of a team are over. If Grit is valued in your culture, you will see Best Effort, Overcoming Adversity, Maturity, and Teamwork as Artifacts. Coaches and athletes will verbally demonstrate their understanding that setbacks and obstacles are necessary to build character. These are opportunities for growth and development that should be embraced. The members of your culture will not complain, and they will deal with the challenges they face by remaining optimistic and committed to the standard that is expected of them. They will work harder.

Real World Example

P.J. Fleck, head coach of the University of Minnesota football team, is known for his strong "row the boat" culture. One key component of his culture is his discernment between "failure" and "failing," which he passes along to his players.[5] In Coach Fleck's eyes, *failing* is when you fall short of your goal and you do not succeed, but instead view your shortcoming as an opportunity for improvement and to succeed in the future.[5] In contrast, *failure* is when you fall short of your goals and you make the conscious decision to give up.[5] Coach Fleck's definitions of these two terms embody the concept of Grit within Legacy Culture. Coming up short of achieving goals is an opportunity to learn and improve.

Why Grit Works

The true colors of a person are revealed not when everything goes their way, but when they face adversity. As a coach, when you speak openly about Grit and frame it in a positive light, your team will follow suit, and common struggles will not become major setbacks because your team will not panic. Setbacks will be viewed as opportunities for triumph and improvement.

INTEGRITY

THE VALUE OF INTEGRITY MEANS that members of the culture hold themselves to the highest moral and ethical standards. Integrity is all about doing everything the right way regardless of whether the result is a win or a loss. It goes beyond the field, court, pool, track, etc. Integrity must be conducted in the classroom and in the personal lives of your athletes. It is a way of life. When the members of your culture buy into holding themselves accountable to Integrity, they will begin to hold each other accountable as members of their team. An element that goes hand in hand with Integrity is personal responsibility. When talking about personal responsibility, it is important to differentiate between *excuses* and *reasons*. *Excuses* defer responsibility, which is evident in the example of "It wasn't my fault, my dog ate my homework." On the other hand, those who provide *reasons* accept personal responsibility and analyze the situation to prevent the error from happening again. For instance, they might say, "It's my fault. I was careless and my dog ate my homework. I will be more aware next time, and I won't let this happen again." Integrity fosters the Artifacts of Transparency, Maturity, Servant Leadership, and Best Effort.

As a coach, you will recognize that Integrity is a Value in your culture when you experience the following Artifacts: players and coaches being honest with one another, never cutting corners, and being more afraid of committing acts of poor sportsmanship than losing. Everyone wants to win, but not at the cost of jeopardizing the character of the team/program/institution/organization. You will never be able to control everything, and you should not want to, but there is no need to worry because results have a way of speaking for themselves. The way your team conducts themselves on the field, in the classroom, and in their personal lives will reveal if there are any issues that are undermining the fabric of the team's integrity.

Real World Example

If one is choosing to live a life of Integrity, Integrity is not something that stands out every once in a while. It becomes the norm. Each day there are fewer examples of Integrity in the news and more examples of unethical behavior because that is what people find interesting. Therefore, it is more fitting to cite an example of the opposite of integrity, such as the corporation Enron, in which its leaders lied, cheated, and stole in order to mislead and manipulate others for personal gain. The Enron story is very popular. Readers can find more information about it very easily should they choose.

Why Integrity Works

Integrity is an essential component of one's character. Whether you are a coach, boss, employee, or athlete, no one can be nor should be micromanaged at all times. That is where Integrity comes in. Coaches need to be able to trust that their athletes are doing what is expected of them when they are not being supervised, and athletes need to trust that coaches are acting in their best interest and in an ethical manner. When Integrity is championed in a culture, the likelihood that acts of deceit and corruption will occur decreases, and should something egregious occur, it will likely be brought to the surface sooner rather than later.

RESPECT

THE VALUE OF RESPECT MEANS that as a member of your team's culture, you respect everyone even if they do not show the same respect back. This means respecting yourself, your teammates, your coaches, opposing teams, fans, and anyone you come into contact with on and off the field. This means that you do not engage in taunting, trash talking, excessive celebrations, or do anything that draws attention to yourself. If the respect you show is not reciprocated, you do not retaliate. You act as the bigger person and turn the other cheek. Instead of opening your mouth, let your actions speak for themselves on the field, court, track, etc. Never turn to social media to take cowardly shots at anyone from behind a screen. Athletes should understand that it is better to say nothing than to say something they will regret. They should exemplify the highest level of sportsmanship. Win or lose, we look our opponents in the eye and shake their hands after engaging in competition. As a coach, you have the ultimate responsibility for not running up the score when your opponent has no realistic chance of winning. The Value of Respect fosters the Artifacts of Camaraderie, Maturity, Servant Leadership, Teamwork, and Class.

As a coach, you will recognize that Respect is a Value in your culture when you experience the following Artifacts: playing with emotion, but not being emotional. To understand the difference, playing with emotion means you care about winning and putting forth your best effort. Being emotional means you are subject to acting impulsively and might let your emotions get the best of you. Picking up an opponent that has fallen. Not running up the score during a victory. Shaking hands after a win or loss. Refraining from trash talk. Remaining calm in situations where your team is provoked.

Real World Examples

Unfortunately, in popular culture it seems like there are more examples of disrespect than respect because disrespectful actions stand out more than those which are respectful. In 2017, New York Giants wide receiver Odell Beckham Jr. portrayed a dog lifting its rear leg to urinate during a touchdown celebration against the Philadelphia Eagles. This behavior was replicated in the 2017 Egg Bowl (the annual Ole Miss–Mississippi State rivalry football game) by D.K. Metcalf, a receiver for the Ole Miss Rebels at the time. It was repeated again by an Ole Miss wide receiver in the 2019 Egg Bowl, and that time it ironically cost them the game because the penalty that ensued resulted in a missed extra point. In 2005, the Michigan State Spartans football team defeated the Notre Dame Fighting Irish, and following the victory, the Michigan State players proceeded to plant their school's flag on the field at Notre Dame stadium. In 2017, following a victory against the Ohio State Buckeyes, Baker Mayfield, quarterback of the Oklahoma Sooners at the time, jogged around the horseshoe and then planted the University of Oklahoma flag on the Ohio Stadium field. In 2018, during the pregame of the Michigan vs. Michigan State football game, Michigan

State players formed a chain and walked across the entire field arm in arm. The problem was, there were Michigan players also on the field warming up. Michigan players stood their ground and moderately aggressively fought through the chain when it passed through them. Some Michigan players viewed this as a sign of disrespect, so Michigan linebacker Devin Bush proceeded to rip up the Michigan State Spartan logo at the center of the field with his cleats. These examples are not meant to portray the perpetrators of these actions as terrible people; they are cited to condemn the behavior, not the individuals. It is these types of behaviors that exemplify poor sportsmanship and are counter to what Legacy Culture stands for.

Now for a positive example of Respect. On one particular occasion during her time of service in Calcutta, India, Saint Teresa of Calcutta asked a baker to provide a starving child with some bread.[6] The baker spat in her face, and she replied, "Thank you for that gift, now do you have something for the child?"[6] Despite being disrespected, Saint Teresa kept her composure and did not lower her standards to the level of the man's despicable behavior. Some individuals may read this example and think that Saint Teresa's response was a sign of weakness, but it is quite the opposite. For her to maintain her composure and not act impulsively takes great strength. And by doing so she was actually standing up to the injustice by not stooping to the same level as the aggressor.

Why Respect Works

Being respectful requires self-control, and self-control is a component of stoicism. In order for a team to become unreactive, they must have discipline. A team with discipline is a team on the path to success. A team that is disciplined will make fewer mistakes and be willing to make the necessary sacrifices to put themselves in the best position to be successful.

FAMILY

THE VALUE OF FAMILY MEANS that teammates, coaches, and administrators genuinely care for one another on and off the field. As a team, you are not only trying to win, but also to improve as leaders and citizens. This requires getting to know one another at a level deeper than the sport you play together. Teammates should help one another as long as they are acting with integrity. They should care for one another and push each other to reach their full potential.

Just as you cannot pick your siblings, you cannot always pick your teammates. You do not have to be best friends with all of your teammates, but you do have to respect them. Any problems that may arise from teammates not behaving accordingly will be and should be addressed as part of your culture. Through the Value of Family, relationships are formed that last long after playing careers are over. The Value of Family fosters the Artifacts of Camaraderie and Teamwork.

As a coach, you will recognize that Family is a Value in your culture when you experience the following Artifacts: coaches having meetings with players to discuss matters relating not only to their sport, but to life in general. Players spending time with one another outside of the time they spend together in games and practice. Experienced leaders reaching out to younger team members to make sure they are included in off-the-field team activities.

Real World Example

Located in Huntingdon, Tennessee, Carroll Academy is a school that offers day-treatment programs for at-risk youth. In May 2013, ESPN did a feature on the Carroll Academy Lady Jags basketball team. The Lady Jags have had a long stretch of struggles on the court, winning only a handful of games over the course of several years, but their team never gave up. Head Coach Randy Hatch and Assistant Coach Patrick Steele understood that the game of basketball is a tool they can use to teach their girls lessons about life. Many of these young women have been dealt difficult circumstances and come from unstable home lives. For them, the Carroll Academy basketball team is their family.

Why Family Works

When a team is built on healthy relationships that go beyond athletics and are grounded in genuine concern for one another's well-being, that team can evolve into a Family. When these relationships are formed, team members are set up to excel in academics and overcome any challenges they may face in their personal lives. Taking on life's challenges alone can be scary for adults, let alone for young people. Having the support of a team makes handling stress and overcoming adversity much easier. In addition, forging strong bonds among team members will improve each member's performance in their athletic domain. A team that cares for one another will work harder for one another.

UNITY

THE VALUE OF UNITY MEANS that as a team, you speak with one voice. This is a reason why social media can work in opposition to the interests of Legacy Culture. It is encouraged that members of Legacy Culture refrain from using social media for personal use in order to avoid potentially putting out content that embarrasses themselves, their families, the team, and the organization or academic institution. A person who is truly devoted to their team and understands the Assumptions and Values of Legacy Culture will understand this and have little difficulty abiding by this suggestion. If members of your team still decide to engage in social media, encourage them to post wholesome content grounded in humility, kindness, and respect. Unity also means that you win and lose as a team. You do not single out teammates and blame them in the event of a loss, unless they have clearly demonstrated a lack of effort or focus. Unity fosters the Artifacts: Camaraderie, Teamwork, and Servant Leadership.

As a coach, you will recognize that Unity is a Value in your culture when you experience the following Artifacts: when a team consisting of administrators, coaches, and players agree on the big things. Team members understand what is expected of them and they behave accordingly.

Real World Example

The Minnesota Golden Gophers football team, helmed by Head Coach P.J. Fleck since 2017, has adopted Fleck's own "row the boat" culture. The success of this culture has produced the fruit of winning seasons. This has only occurred because the players have bought into the culture. If the players were not invested in Coach Fleck's program, the team would not be having the success they have experienced.

Why Unity Works

Strategies can only be effective when they are well executed, and for a sports team or a company to execute a strategy well requires the athletes or employees to buy into it. When this occurs, Unity is formed because the team or company believes in the direction in which they are headed—in other words, they can see the big picture. Any team or close-knit group of people can afford to disagree on the little things, the details that may differ but are still in line with the overall direction in which they are headed. However, when there is disagreement regarding the bigger picture, pertaining to the overall beliefs and direction of the team, group, company etc., this is a recipe for dysfunction and will most likely inhibit the individuals from coming together to maximize their potential and achieve success.

HUMILITY

THE VALUE OF HUMILITY MEANS that members of Legacy Culture understand that they would not be successful without their teammates and coaches. As a result, team members behave unselfishly and are reluctant to take personal credit when they are praised. It has become popular in college football to reward defensive players when they force a turnover with some type of accessory they can wear that is flashy and makes them stand out. Members of a culture that has adopted the Legacy Culture framework do not need this type of motivation to perform at their role. They understand that when they do something positive, they find themselves in that position with the help of their teammates. Therefore, one person never deserves all of the credit. Instead, the focus is on the team.

There is only one type of acceptable celebration: one that is conducted with humility. When a player scores, they should simply go about business as usual like a true champion. They should hand the ball to the official and embrace their teammates while they head back to the appropriate sideline. Humble athletes do not trash talk, showboat, or taunt. When they score, they avoid doing anything that would draw additional attention to themselves. Unfortunately, in some sports it is common to see players engage in premediated solo or group celebrations, perhaps because they want to stand out and be remembered. When these types of celebrations occur, fans remember them for a few days, but they are soon forgotten. It is ironic, because for a player to have a truly memorable moment would actually require the exact opposite of them. Humility goes a long way and teams and athletes are remembered for it. The problem with what some people may consider to be "harmless" excessive celebrations are that they have a ripple effect. When young children see professional athletes celebrate excessively, they begin to think this is what the game is all about and will model this type of behavior.

One of the greatest traditions in all of sports is the handshakes that take place at the end of each series in the Stanley Cup playoffs. Trash talking and fighting is an element of hockey, but maintaining a level of respect where you have the class to shake the hand of your opponent regardless of whether or not you like or dislike them personally is something that should be praised and adopted by all sports. We can all learn something from this great hockey tradition.

As a coach, you will recognize that Humility is a Value in your culture when you experience the following Artifacts: no taunting, trash talking, or showboating. Players giving credit to others for their success and avoiding anything that would put them in the spotlight unnecessarily. Picking up opponents that have fallen and respectfully shaking hands with them after competition. As a coach or player, you will know Humility is a Value in your team's culture when the best players on your team refuse to acknowledge their individual success. They attribute their success to the help of their teammates and coaches while putting the team before themselves.

Real World Examples

One of the themes of Legacy Culture is not desiring the spotlight for personal glory. Sia, the musical artist well-known for covering her face with a wig, desired to pursue her love of music, but she did not want to take on the consequences that come with fame. By obscuring her face with a bold wig, she is indicating that she desires to be out of the spotlight, even though it may try to find her. It is this attitude of not seeking attention that sets the standard for what it means to be humble in Legacy Culture. This is not to say that everyone must go to the extreme of hiding their face with a wig, but it gets the point across that personal pride is not an element of the Legacy Culture framework. An excellent example of Humility can be seen in athlete interviews, when a reporter praises the player for their success only to have the athlete respond by saying, "It is not about me, it is about the team and the organization. We all did it together."

Why Humility Works

The Value of Humility is centered upon living an unselfish life. A life that puts others at the center of it. Living a life committed to serving others leads to living a life of great meaning. A meaningful life is a life of lasting happiness, which leads to a life full of joy. When team members are grounded in Humility, they can achieve great things together that they otherwise would not be able to achieve by themselves.

LEADING BY EXAMPLE

THE VALUE OF LEADING BY EXAMPLE means that everyone has the opportunity to be a leader by exemplifying the behaviors promoted by Legacy Culture. As part of the Legacy Culture framework, having seniority does not mean delegating chores to underclassmen. As you get older and become more experienced, you must take on more responsibility because you need to demonstrate to the younger team members what it truly means to be a leader. It is acceptable to delegate as long as the leaders and senior members of the team are getting their hands dirty themselves. As you advance into the position of a senior leader, you do not get to kick back and watch everyone else work. You must become the definition of a servant leader. Put others before yourself and do not ask anyone to do anything you would not be willing to do yourself. The Value of Leading by Example fosters all of the Artifacts of Legacy Culture.

As a coach, you will recognize that Leading by Example is a Value in your culture when you experience the following Artifacts: Upperclassmen and veteran players exemplifying what it means to be a standout member of the team, institution, or organization. Arriving early and staying late to put in the extra work. Setting up equipment with the younger members of the team before and after practice. Accepting and embracing that leadership and experience come with more responsibility.

Real World Examples

In 2017, after a long rain delay, the Penn State Nittany Lions football team gave up a fourth-quarter lead, losing to the Michigan State Spartans by a field goal as time expired, and ending their Big Ten championship and College Football Playoff hopes. The defeat was devastating to the Penn State players, coaches, and fans. Immediately following the conclusion of the game, some Penn State players headed straight for the locker room. This caught the attention of head coach James Franklin. From the television screen, Coach Franklin could be seen sprinting after his players yelling at them to get their attention and demanding that they go back to shake hands with players of the opposing team. Coach Franklin's energy and commitment to not letting his team stoop to a level below his program's standard exemplifies what it means to Lead by Example and hold others accountable to stand up for what is right. Even if it means making a scene.

George Washington, Abraham Lincoln, Mahatma Gandhi, Winston Churchill, Nelson Mandela, Martin Luther King Jr., Saint Teresa of Calcutta . . . the list goes on and on. These historical figures and many others gained a multitude of followers by demonstrating the courage to stand up for their beliefs through the way they lived their lives.

Why Leading by Example Works

It's very simple. When someone is not willing to live up to the expectations they hold others to, they lose the respect and trust of others. Leaders who take action inspire others to follow suit by their own example.

SERVICE

THE VALUE OF SERVICE IS an integral part of Legacy Culture. Team members must understand that being a member of a team is a platform to do good and make a difference in the community. This Value helps instill in young people a desire to give back and do good throughout the course of their lives. Teams should find time to give back on a regular basis as opposed to one-time community service activities. Volunteering consistently allows individuals to derive a stronger sense of purpose and cherish the investment of the work they have put in. It allows for team bonding and serves as a reminder that service to others is an essential component to living a meaningful life. However, it is important that the service not be completed out of personal pride. Everyone involved in service should refrain from drawing attention to their good deeds in a way that gives them personal credit. If a camera captures a good deed that was not intended to be filmed by the individual performing the deed, then the service was not performed out of vanity. But if the individual performing the good deed intentionally tries to make the action public knowledge in a way that draws attention to themselves, then vanity is at play and the act was not done in the spirit of pure service. The Value of Service fosters the Artifacts of Community Service and Leading by Example.

As a coach, you will recognize that Service is a Value of your culture when you experience the following Artifacts in your culture: administrators, coaches, and players participating in a service activity they are passionate about on a consistent basis.

Real World Examples

Service activities that can be done in groups or individually include: cleaning up parts of the community, serving at soup kitchens, visiting hospitals, and volunteering with youth organizations, food banks, prisons, and other charities.

Why Service Works

Service is a critical component of a team that desires to embrace the Legacy Culture framework. It is the Value that complements the foundation of Legacy Culture, which includes the Assumptions of being Ethical and Selfless. When you give back to the community and do something nice for others, even if you are not thanked directly, there is still a great sense of purpose and meaning to be experienced. Legacy Culture is about taking responsibility and demonstrating leadership in a way that leaves the world better off than when you found it. The Value of Service teaches young men and women how to live their lives long after their athletic career is over. It is not subject to a time clock or a finish line. There are always more problems to solve, more lives to touch, and more charitable acts required to spread kindness and prosperity throughout the world.

SACRIFICE

IT IS EVIDENT FROM ALL of the Values that Legacy Culture promotes that this framework is not for everyone. It is not a shortcut or an easy path to follow. To live a life rooted in Legacy Culture requires sacrifices. Therefore, Sacrifice is not a deliberate value of the culture, rather it is a necessary byproduct in order to be successful. Sacrifice is unique in that it can also take the form of an Artifact by taking part in the act of sacrificing instant gratification for long-term success. Athletes in a culture that has adopted Legacy Culture understand and are willing to give up anything that may give them instant gratification in order to reap long-term happiness and benefits.

As a coach, you will recognize that Sacrifice is a Value in your culture when you experience the following Artifacts in your culture: Members of your culture are maintaining healthy diets, refraining from social media use or using it responsibly, getting enough sleep, abstaining from excessive alcohol, performing well in the classroom, and avoiding situations where it is expected that temptations will arise.

Real World Examples

It is difficult to list mainstream examples of sacrifices teams make to achieve excellence because for the most part they go unnoticed by the media. Everyone wants to be on the podium holding the trophy at the end of it all, but they do not see the work that went into getting there. It is not a secret that Olympic athletes, especially young Olympic athletes, live very unique lives compared to their peers. They spend hours each day practicing their craft in a regimented manner. They sacrifice the luxuries that most people in America indulge in and consider to be "normal" aspects of their everyday lives. All of which relate to the diet and lifestyles of these athletes.

Why Sacrifice Works

The more work we put into something, the more we appreciate the work for what it is. In most cases, sacrifices must be made in order to achieve a preferred result because the desired outcome is difficult to achieve. There is much truth to the saying: "if it were easy, everyone would do it." Sacrifice requires discipline, discipline is necessary to achieve commitment, and commitment leads to sustained excellence.

ARTIFACTS

The Artifacts of a culture are the tangible manifestations of the Assumptions and Values.[1]

TRANSPARENCY

PRACTICING OPEN COMMUNICATION AMONG ATHLETES, coaches, and administration. If you are not doing anything wrong, then you have nothing to hide. When you see something happening that is illegal or frowned upon, it is addressed. Issues are not covered up for fear of consequences.

CAMARADERIE

DEVELOPING STRONG LIFELONG RELATIONSHIPS ACROSS all levels of the program. Genuinely caring for one another in public and private life while maintaining boundaries out of respect for one another.

BEST EFFORT

UNDERSTANDING AND ACCEPTING THAT THERE will be good and bad days. It is not expected to maintain a record-breaking performance continually, day in and day out. It is expected that performance will fluctuate a little, but everyone will put their energy and focus into getting better each day, holding nothing back.

OVERCOMING ADVERSITY

OVERCOMING CHALLENGES THAT ONCE STOOD in your way. Individuals coming together as a team to find a way to come out on top.

COMMUNITY SERVICE

PARTICIPATING IN ACTIVITIES THAT HAVE the potential to change the lives of those who may be less fortunate. Understanding that giving back and helping others is ultimately more important than participating in the sport that brought your team together. The program you are part of is a powerful platform that can be used to help others.

MATURITY

LEADING BY EXAMPLE AND DEMONSTRATING the highest level of sportsmanship. Making the necessary sacrifices that come with Legacy Culture in order to be successful.

TEAMWORK

UNDERSTANDING THAT MEMBERS of a team are stronger together than they are individually. Athletes are willing to give up personal glory so that their team may win. They are willing to embrace working with one another to achieve common goals.

SERVANT LEADERSHIP

LEADING BY EXAMPLE AND PUTTING others before oneself. Not being afraid to be the first to take on and embrace responsibility.

DISCIPLINE

MAKING SACRIFICES IN YOUR PERSONAL life in order to live up to the expectations of the Legacy Culture framework.

CLASS

SHOWING RESPECT TO EVERYONE AND demonstrating the highest level of sportsmanship. Refraining from trash talk and letting actions speak louder than words.

DEALING WITH SOCIAL MEDIA

AS A DISCLAIMER, THE LEGACY CULTURE framework takes a strong stance on social media. Coaches are welcome to disagree with the following viewpoint, but it cannot be understated that social media plays a large part in the culture of the greater society and as a result has an influence on your team's culture. Social media is a complicated issue interwoven with the technology of the world today. An entire book covering social media would not be enough to address the complicated issues social media presents and the pros and cons of its utilization. Therefore, this book will not attempt to cover all aspects of social media and how they affect teams and cultures. Instead, it will present a foundation with which to approach social media, which coaches and leaders can use at their discretion.

Earlier it was stated that coaches should encourage athletes to practice responsible social media use or avoid it all together. Coaches should not force their athletes to give up social media; rather they should warn them about its dangers and encourage responsible use. Athletes must make the decision to stay off social media for themselves. Social media, just like all other forms of technology, is a tool. Whether that tool is used positively or negatively is at the discretion of the individual operating it.

Social media has become a window into the lives of its users. Users often post highly personal pictures, videos, and thoughts in the form of text-based quotes. This practice has become a way of life for some, and the posts are often fired off impulsively. As human beings, we all make mistakes and at times act impulsively on our emotions by saying or doing things we regret after the fact. However, when you throw social media into the conversation and your flaws and mistakes are etched into the stone of the digital world for millions to see, this changes everything. For example, in 2018, Braylon Edwards, a former University of Michigan football player and Big Ten Network commentator at the time, was suspended from his position with the Big Ten Network for posting a tweet containing profanity in which he expressed his disgust for the performance of his alma mater after a loss to the University of Notre Dame. Braylon did not do anything egregious. To be honest, his statement was a normal reaction for someone who is by nature competitive, feeling upset, and deeply cares for their alma mater. However, his comment was inappropriate for a sports television analyst to publicly make and unfortunately, it affected his employment situation. If he had kept his comment to himself or portrayed his feelings in an appropriate manner, the entire situation could have been avoided. There are countless examples that can easily be found from an internet search of social media posts that cost people their jobs or got them into trouble one way or another. Granted, a lot of the examples of what people post are written out of impulsive carelessness, but the point is there is no reason crude content needs to be posted in the first place. Social media can be highly personal, but it is also largely a false reality. It makes sense that people only post good things about their lives and flattering pictures of themselves.

There are many negative effects of using social media:

It is addictive.[4]

- The amount of research in this area is steadily increasing. Just look around in a public area and you will see almost everyone glued to their phones.

It can be frivolous.

- Take some time to reflect and evaluate the content you view on social media. Ask yourself, "Is this improving my life or holding me back?"

It can be vain.[4]

- This is the strongest argument against social media use for Legacy Culture. Vanity is the enemy of humility.

It risks an invasion of privacy.

- It is the instinct of young people today to pull out their phones and film something that they find worthy of their social media accounts. Not everything is meant to be nor should be filmed and posted on the internet.

It can contribute to anxiety and depression among young people.[4]

- Research indicates that higher instances of anxiety and depression diagnosed in young people can be linked to increased social media use.

It leaves you unable to enjoy the moment.

- Today people are so concerned about taking the perfect picture or video that they cannot enjoy a moment for what it is worth. Technology longs for our attention and is very successful at attaining it, which can oftentimes rob us of the present moment.

For the purposes of Legacy Culture, the worst effect of social media is vanity. Vanity is defined as "excessive pride in one's appearance, qualities, achievements, etc." We all have different blessings in our lives—a well-paying job, a beautiful family, a beautiful home, a nice car, loving pets, family vacations, etc.—and these are great things that are not inherently bad. However, when we take pictures of the great things we have going for us in our lives and post them to social media for countless people to see, we can be engaging in vanity without even realizing it. This creates a false reality for social media users and can elicit feelings of anxiety and depression among them. It is also a catalyst for envy. In most cases, there is absolutely no reason of substance that exists for why personal photos have to be posted to social media. It is most often done purely for social recognition and attention to establish the user's prominence as a desirable individual with a social life. The antidote to this problem is simple: live a private life.

Now you may be thinking, how does this affect me as a coach? The answer is that Humility is the most important Value as part of Legacy Culture, and Vanity and Humility are in opposition. A vain person says, "Look at me, look at how happy I am and all the success I've had." While the humble person says, "I am thankful for my success, but I do not want any extra attention. It's not about me. It's about the team." As a coach, your team will experience success and your players may experience individual success. Encourage your athletes to live private lives. Warn them about the relationship between vanity and social media use.

Invasion of privacy is the second crucial reason to avoid social media within your culture. There is a difference between privacy and secrecy. As a coach utilizing the Legacy Culture framework, you want to create a culture where transparency uncovers any unethical activities, but this does not mean everything must be public or there is no privacy. In 2019, following Louisiana State University's win over the University of Alabama in football, LSU's head football coach Ed Orgeron addressed his team in the locker room and used some profanity. Coach Orgeron never intended for his words to leave the locker room, but one of Orgeron's players was on his phone using social media and recorded Orgeron's words. The statement that was never intended to leave the locker room was heard by millions of people and caught the attention of sports news. The line between private and public has become blurred because of social media and it is unacceptable. To avoid these issues on your team, you must drive home the message of humility, warn against vanity, and emphasize the importance of privacy. Especially in sensitive areas like a locker room.

Overall, social media use is a complicated issue. As a coach, you cannot expect to monitor or control your athletes' use of social media in its entirety. Once again, this is not meant to cover every aspect of social media use. However, addressing social media in your team's culture does not need to be complicated. Simply do the following:

- WARN YOUR ATHLETES OF THE DANGERS AND DOWNSIDES OF SOCIAL MEDIA DISCUSSED IN THIS BOOK.

- IF YOUR ATHLETES CHOOSE TO USE SOCIAL MEDIA, CHALLENGE THEM TO ASK THEMSELVES BEFORE POSTING CONTENT, "IS THIS POST GROUNDED IN HUMILITY AND KINDNESS?" IF THE ANSWER IS NO, THE CONTENT SHOULD NOT BE POSTED.

- ENCOURAGE YOUR PLAYERS TO LIVE A PRIVATE LIFE (ONCE AGAIN COMING BACK TO THE IDEA OF HUMILITY).

- LEAD BY EXAMPLE. EITHER HAVE NO SOCIAL MEDIA PRESENCE OR HAVE ONE GROUNDED IN HUMILITY AND KINDNESS. DO NOT SEEK UNNECESSARY ATTENTION AND STRIVE TO LIVE A PRIVATE LIFE.

FORGIVENESS AND DISCIPLINE

AS MOST TEAMS AND ORGANIZATIONS already practice, there needs to be consequences for rule breaking. This is especially true when utilizing the Legacy Culture framework in order to hold everyone accountable and maintain a standard of excellence. When a violation of the rules occurs, the appropriate disciplinary actions must be taken regardless of who commits the violation. As previously mentioned, Legacy Culture is a platform to make a difference in people's lives. This can take place both outside and inside of your program. It cannot be overstated that athletic teams have the ability to greatly alter the course of a person's life for the better. Therefore, when someone violates team rules (depending on the severity of their actions), it is recommended that they should be given a second chance to be a part of the team. This should involve the athlete in violation of the rules having the opportunity to serve their punishment and then prove themselves as a productive member of the team who is willing to contribute to the health of the culture.

CONCLUDING THOUGHTS

CHANGE IS NOT EASY, AND implementing a culture change takes time. If you are a leader who wishes to embark on the journey of adopting the Legacy Culture framework, you must understand that cultural changes do not happen instantaneously. You cannot set a deadline saying you will have adopted it by a certain date. Legacy Culture is a lifestyle, and lifestyles never end. My hope for anyone utilizing Legacy Culture is not to become frustrated or overwhelmed by the details when you face hard times. Instead, never forget the ultimate purpose of the Legacy Culture framework: to develop young men and women so they may grow up and conduct themselves with the highest level of integrity while striving to make the world a better place for their fellow people.

Thank you!

BIBLIOGRAPHY

1. Schein, E. H. (2010). *Organizational Culture and Leadership*. San Francisco: Jossey-Bass.

2. Beer, M., Eisenstat, R. A., & Spector, B. (1990). "Why Change Programs Don't Produce Change." Harvard Business Review. 177–197.

3. Duckworth, A. (2016). *Grit: The power of passion and perseverance*. New York: Scribner/Simon & Schuster.

4. Walton, Alice G, "6 Ways Social Media Affects Our Mental Health," Forbes, June 13, 2017.

5. GopherAthletics. "Gopher Talk 101 with P.J. Fleck: 'Failing vs. Failure.'" YouTube, 28 Apr. 2017, www.youtube.com/watch?v=oq3ji-Urg7vY&ab_channel=MinnesotaGophers.

6. Barron, R. (2011). *Catholicism: A Journey to the Heart of the Faith*. Image Books.

APPENDIX A

Diagnosing Your Culture

Answer the following questions to analyze your culture and gain a strong understanding of its different elements.

1. List up to five adjectives that you believe describe your current culture.

2. In your opinion, what are the Assumptions (the beliefs so engrained in the members of a culture they are taken for granted) of your current culture?

3. In your opinion, what are the Values (the beliefs, goals, or ideals of the members of the culture that may or may not manifest) of your current culture?

4. In your opinion, what are the Artifacts (the tangible manifestations of the Artifacts and Values that appeal to the five senses, i.e., behaviors, apparel, technology, tools, and procedures) in your current culture?

APPENDIX B

Changing Your Culture

1. What do you want the Assumptions of your culture to be?

2. What do you want the Values of your culture to be?

3. What do you want the Artifacts of your culture to be?

4. As a leader of your culture, what steps do you need to take to establish these Artifacts in your culture?

Outline of Legacy Culture

Assumptions	Values	Artifacts
Love of the Game	Legacy	All
	Positive Attitude	Camaraderie Best Effort Overcoming Adversity Maturity Teamwork
Desire to Become the Best Version of Yourself	Work Ethic	Best Effort Overcoming Adversity
	Grit	Best Effort Overcoming Adversity Maturity Teamwork
Ethical	Integrity	Transparency Maturity Servant Leadership Best Effort
	Respect	Camaraderie Maturity Servant Leadership Teamwork Class
Selfless	Family	Camaraderie Teamwork
	Unity	Camaraderie Teamwork Servant Leadership
	Humility	Camaraderie Best Effort Maturity Teamwork Servant Leadership Discipline
	Sacrifice	Camaraderie Maturity Servant Leadership Teamwork Discipline

ABOUT THE AUTHOR

RONALD MONACK attained a bachelor of science in psychology in 2017 from Saint Vincent College in Latrobe, Pennsylvania. He went on to complete a master's degree in management and operational excellence from Saint Vincent College in August 2018. His passion for studying organizational culture and human behavior inspired him to design the Legacy Culture. Legacy Culture was formed through his experiences as an athlete and a coach. In high school, Ronald participated on the cross country, basketball, and track and field teams. He went on to compete at the division three collegiate level in cross country and track and field at Saint Vincent College. He now enjoys coaching various sports at a variety of age levels.

There is an epidemic of poor sportsmanship in our culture, and this is a challenge that Ronald is ambitiously willing take on. It is his hope that *Legacy Culture* will have the power to change lives by developing young men and women into ethical leaders within their communities, striving to make a lasting positive change in the world.